A Wife's Daily Prayer Confession

31 DAYS OF POWERFUL, LIFE CHANGING CONFESSIONS

Treshelle Williams

A Wife's Daily Prayer Confession

ISBN: 978-0-9992230-0-0

Acknowledgement

Jesus declared that “It is finished” after hours of pain and turmoil on the cross. Though my life and mission pale in comparison, I can say the same. Two years have elapsed, and I have finally completed the goal of releasing my first book of Confessions. This accomplishment would not have been possible without the support of the Wife Talk Team. God has surrounded me with an abundance of talented, skilled, loving, and dedicated women that have consistently worked diligently to bring the vision to fruition. Without them, there would be no Wife Talk, or “A Wife’s Daily Confession” book. For months, they have encouraged me until the book was complete. And for that, I say thank you to my awesome Wife Talk Team. You are all the best!

Thank you to each of my unseen mentors, who taught me the importance of confessing God's word over my life daily. These Confessions were birthed from sitting at your feet learning and growing. I am forever thankful for that.

Finally, a special and huge thank you goes to my husband. Tony, you have supported me through ‘thick and thin.’ It has not always been smooth sailing, but we made it to the finish line. Thank you for encouraging me, and for your unconditional love during the entire process. I love you.

Dedication

A life without guidance is a life I never want to live. I am honored to dedicate this book to every Pastor, Leader and Teacher that challenged me to grow and stretch far beyond what I thought capable. Some of you I have had the honor of working with directly, and others I followed with pen and paper as if you were giving me the secrets to life (and you were). My voice is your voice, and your voice will forever stay imprinted on my heart. Thank you for being the forrunner in this race of life and grace.

Preface

‘A Wife's Daily Prayer Confession” was birthed from a desire to help wives and engaged women to speak life into every area of their lives; specifically, over their marriage and husbands. In a world where the announcement of marriage is quickly followed by the option of divorce, my heart’s desire is to help change the narrative of what we speak. My passion is to teach women that if they speak what they see, they will continue to have what they say.

I challenge you to change what you are saying so that you can change what you are seeing! As Children of God, we have the power and authority to speak, declare and decree. And it is our right to have what we say. My goal in starting this journey was to create a tribe of women that would rather speak to their mountains, troubles and frustrations, than about them. I wanted wives to understand that our words are powerful and that we can use them to build up our marriages or tear them down.

I declare over the Wife Tribe that they shall chose life and life more abundant - until it is full with over-flow.

Prayer Confessions

Table of Contents

Anger

In the name of Jesus, I declare I walk boldly in my covenant rights with God. I have the peace of God; therefore, I am whole and complete in every area. I declare; peace guides me to God's favor and activates God's promise in my life. I declare; nothing is missing or broken in my life. My peace in God provides me the reassurance that I am empowered by God to succeed in everything I do.

Thank you, Lord, I declare I will follow your example to be merciful and gracious, slow to anger and plenteous in mercy and love, forgiveness, and kindness (Ex.34:6). I will walk in temperance all the days of my life.

I declare I will have great patience and understanding in all circumstances and situations

(Col. 3:12). I will never act or respond out of emotions or fear. I declare I will not be like those who are hasty in spirit, exploding in destruction with words and actions (Prov. 14:29). But I will tame my upset and anger by continually being led by the Holy Spirit.

Thank you, Lord, that I will operate in your word because I know a soft answer turns away wrath (Prov. 15:1). I declare I am not hot tempered, easily offended, quick with wrong words, or unable to see sound reason and understanding. I declare when I am angry, I do not sin or let my wrath, my exasperation, my fury or indignation last long. I release anger and frustration quickly. (Ep 4:26)

Thank you, Lord, I will not let bitterness, wrath, rage, a bad temper, resentment, quarreling, or slander be a part of my character or person. I will become useful and helpful and kind to other with a tender heart and compassion, even as I forgive those who may have wronged me. (Col 3:8)

Thank you **L**ord for helping me get rid of all things that are not like you; anger, hateful feeling, and wrong thinking. And I replace those negative with a positive. I will be loving, understanding, kind, tender hearted, and always forgiving (Ep. 4:32).

I receive your help and your love in this area right now in Jesus' name. Amen

Notes:

Depression

In the name of Jesus, I declare I walk boldly in my covenant rights with God. I have the peace of God; therefore, I am whole and complete in every area. I declare; peace guides me to God's favor and activates God's promise in my life. I declare; nothing is missing or broken in my life. My peace in God provides me the reassurance that I am empowered by God to succeed in everything I do.

Father in the name of Jesus, I thank you for going before me and preparing a place for me that will be great (John 14:1-31). Thank you lord that depression is not a part of my Godly Character that you have given me and I declare I have the right to cast it down and send it to hell for it to never come to me again (Matt. 25:41).

Thank you Lord for always being my shield, my glory, and the lifter of my head. (Ps. 3:3) Thank you Father for never leaving me nor forsaking me, even in my low moments (Heb. 13:5). I declare that the eyes of the lord are on me, and his ears are open to my cry. When I cry out, the Lord hears and delivers me out of all my trouble. (Ps. 34:15, 17)

I confess, when my soul is cast down within me, I remember the Lord and his goodness to me. Thank you, Lord, for your loving kindness at all times.

Satan, in the Name of Jesus, I rebuke your attempts to twist my thoughts, feelings, and emotions concerning my life, family, husband and myself. I am a child of the most high God and you have no right to any part of my life, not even my thought life. SO, I say to you right now, take your spirit of depression, hurt, and feelings of shame back to the pit of hell with you. You cannot live in my mind, heart, or spirit. And you surly can't live in my house or among my family (James 4:7).

Thank you, Lord, for the spirit of depression I replace it with a spirit of Joy, Peace, Love, and fruitfulness! Thank you father for giving me your right spirit in me (Ps. 51:10). Because I have set my love upon you Lord, You have delivered me and have set me on high and shown me your great mercy, love and kindness. (Ps. 42: 6, 8, 11)

I declare and decree right now, depression you can never live in me again!

In Jesus' Name Amen.

Notes:

____

____

____

____

____

____

____

____

Faith

In the name of Jesus, I declare I walk boldly in my covenant rights with God. I have the peace of God; therefore, I am whole and complete in every area. I declare; peace guides me to God's favor and activates God's promise in my life. I declare; nothing is missing or broken in my life. My peace in God provides me the reassurance that I am empowered by God to succeed in everything I do.

I declare, God's Word is alive in me and great manifestation is showing up now as I speak. God speaks to me through His Word daily and my Faith is feed by the word of God. Thank you father for giving me revelation knowledge through your word (Ps. 119:66).

I confess and declare that your word is true. I believe God's Word and a voice of another I will never follow (John 10:27). I declare, I walk in the light of God's word daily and that word watches over me to perform goodness all the days of my life.

I declare, I am redeemed from the curse of the law and I walk in faith to accomplish everything that God has placed in my heart to accomplish (Gal. 3:13). Today, my Faith affords me the ability to have a sound mind and fear cannot sway me. I stand in faith, knowing that every good work that has begun in me will be performed until the day of Jesus Christ (Phil. 1:6).

Thank you, Father. You have made me able to partake of my inheritance goodness, peace, prosperity, and favor now. I declare my faith allows me to say to every mountain in my life, move, be gone, and it shall go away. I listen to the Word of God, and faith comes to me (Matt. 17:20).

The Word, God's Word, the word of faith, is near me. I hide it in my heart. I declare and I speak it with my mouth. My word will produce faith that can be seen clearly in my life. My faith and action changes things. I hold my desired results in my thoughts until I see it in my hands. My faith grows exceedingly. I feed my faith on the Word of God. I exercise my faith daily and I put it to practice. My faith increases daily. My faith is strong. My faith is measuring up to great faith, rich faith, perfect faith, unfeigned faith, overcoming faith. I am full of faith!

I live by the Word of God, I feed my faith daily. I mediate on it day and night. I declare as I feed my spirit man, I grow stronger. Faith is my Spiritual Food. My faith rest in God's Word! I study the Word of God regularly and my faith grows stronger because of it. According to my faith be it unto me. I am using my faith today to receive God's promises in my life. I declare I am Faithful and I am the child of the most High God. I am exercising my faith. I am putting my faith into practice to bring great results into my life. My faith always works (Rom. 1:17).

Today, I declare I will forever trust the Lord with all my heart. I will not lean to my own understanding (Prov. 3:5) and I will acknowledge Him in all my ways, for I know he will always direct my path. I declare my heart is fixed on God's Word and what he says, it is true. I am not faithless; I am a believer only! I believe according to God's Word, regardless of what I see, hear or feel (Heb. 11:1). I am the faithful child of a faithful God. I imitate my Father. My actions are his action, He is my example while I am on this earth. I act in faith. I call those things which be not as though they were. And I declare they will manifest right before me (Rom. 4:17).

I am fully persuaded that what God has promised, He is able to perform. I can give glory to God. I am strong in faith because I am strong in God's Word. I have the Abraham-kind of faith. I have mountain moving faith. I have the God kind of faith (Gen. 15:6).

My prayers work. My faith works by love. I do not permit unforgiveness into my being. I refuse to hold ought against anyone. I can forgive. I am quick to forgive. And my Father in heaven forgives me (Mark 11:25).

I let the love of God that has been shed abroad in my heart by the Holy Spirit dominate me. I have what I say. I release my faith in God's words (Rom. 5:5). In Jesus Name, Amen!

Notes:

Family

In the name of Jesus, I declare I walk boldly in my covenant rights with God. I have the peace of God; therefore, I am whole and complete in every area. I declare; peace guides me to God's favor and activates God's promise in my life. I declare; nothing is missing or broken in my life. My peace in God provides me the reassurance that I am empowered by God to succeed in everything I do.

In the name of Jesus, I pray and confess Your Word over my entire family this morning, my husband, my parents, siblings, grandparents, cousins, and any member under the family umbrella. I declare that this day, they are surrounded with the faith of Your word father and your many blessings.

I declare that they are WHOLE with nothing missing, broken, or lacking in their lives today.

Thank you, Father, that my faith in the Word of God covers them and You watch over it to perform your word!

I boldly confess and believe that every family member is disciples of Christ taught of the Lord and obedient to Gods will. Thank you lord that great is the peace of my children and my family. Thank you lord that they honor, esteem, and value your word, and this brings them long life (Deut. 5:33).

Thank you Lord for contending with that which pertains with my family and You give them safety and ease all the days of their life.

I declare that You are more than enough lord to fix any situation in their lives! Every family member, those distant and near is healthy, healed, and with nothing missing or broken in their lives (Phil.4:19).

Thank you, Lord, they obey your word and the voice of another they WILL NOT follow. Thank you, Father, they have all come to the knowledge of you. Those unsaved, I call them into the body of Christ NOW, in Jesus name.

Lord, I believe and confess that You give Your angels charge over my family to accompany, defend, and preserve them in all their ways (Ps. 91:11). You, Lord, are their refuge and fortress. You are their glory and the lifter of his heads (Ps. 3:3).

Father, I confess that You will perfect that which concerns me. I commit and cast the care of my family once and for all over on you, Father (1 Peter 5:7). They are in Your hands, and I am positively persuaded that You are able to guard and keep that which I have committed to You. (1 John 4:14-15).

In Jesus Name, Amen.

Notes:

____

____

____

____

____

Notes:

Finances: Debt-Free

In the name of Jesus, I declare I walk boldly in my covenant rights with God. I have the peace of God; therefore, I am whole and complete in every area. I declare; peace guides me to God's favor and activates God's promise in my life. I declare; nothing is missing or broken in my life. My peace in God provides me the reassurance that I am empowered by God to succeed in everything I do.

In Jesus' name, I declare I am debt - free! The spirit of debt and financial bondage is completely demolished over my life and over the lives of my family. No longer will I operate in bondage to debt and financial hardship because I have renewed my mind in the word of god and I have actively changed my spending habits.

Thank you, Lord, for supernatural insight of how to effective handle finances. I declare I am capable, knowledgeable, and a good steward over the wealth and riches you placed in my house. Thank you Lord my husband and I increase more and more every day in knowledge, your word, and our finances. We give generously, and it is given back to us with increase. Debt and financial bondage can't live in our presence (2 Cor. 9:7).

Thank you, God, for giving me the power to get wealth to establish your kingdom here in the earth and to leave a legacy of greatness for our children's children. Thank you, Lord, that my husband and I are established as the lender and not the borrower, we are the head and not the tail (Deut. 15:6; Deut. 28:13). We are blessed coming in and blessed going out. Thank you Lord for debt freedom now.

I declare, the Father daily loads us with benefits and causes the Lords blessings to overtake us (Deut.28:2). Thank you

Lord that you have given my husband and I richly all things to enjoy. I declare, the blessing of the Lord has made us rich, adding no sorrow with it.

Thank you Lord that we are joint heirs with Jesus Christ and Abraham's blessings belong to us (Romans 8:17). My husband and I sow bountifully, therefore, we reap bountifully. We give and it is given unto us.

Thank you, Lord, we have the authority in our mouth to rebuke the devourer and any attempts there are of Satan to steal, kill, or destroy our finances or the fruit of our hands (Mal. 3:11). God's promises are ours, and I receive them NOW by faith (2 Cor. 5:7). I declare and decree that wealth and riches is mine now. They are a part of my life without working like a slave. Debt must go now, in Jesus name. I command it to never return.

I stand steadfast, unmovable on the promise of God (1 Cor. 15:58). And I am set in my heart trusting that God will bring every promise to pass. No debt in my house, my family, or in my business. In Jesus Name. I am Debt Free; my husband and Family is debt free. In Jesus' Name, Amen.

Notes:

____

____

____

____

____

Finances: Favor

In the name of Jesus, I declare I walk boldly in my covenant rights with God. I have the peace of God; therefore, I am whole and complete in every area. I declare; peace guides me to God's favor and activates God's promise in my life. I declare; nothing is missing or broken in my life. My peace in God provides me the reassurance that I am empowered by God to succeed in everything I do.

In the Name of Jesus, I am the righteousness of God and Favor is my covenant right as a child of God (2 Cor. 5:21). I declare I am surrounded and engulf with covenant kindness and favor all the days of my life. Favor chases me down and seeks after me. Thank you, Father, for your favor that you have so richly given to me.

I declare the favor of God activates sweat-less increase in my life. My husband and I see the favor of God on our jobs, in the stores we visit, and in ever place our feet shall tread. I declare that God's Favor on my life is the secret ingredient to all my success. Success on my job, in my business, and in every place, I show up.

Because I am the righteousness of God, I declare I see the manifestation of God's favor on my life daily. FAVOR surrounds me everywhere I go and in everything I do. I expect the favor of God to be in full manifestation in my life every day.

I declare never again will I show up without the cover of God's favor on me. Favor rests upon me and my husband. It produces great results for us and all around us. I declare immeasurable, limitless, and surpassing favor in the lives of my husband, children, and family. We shall see the fruit of favor daily.

Thank you **F**ather I declare that your favor produces supernatural increase, promotion, restoration, honor, increased assets, greater victories, recognition, preferential treatment, petitions granted, policies and rules changed FOR ME, and every battle won in which I do not have to fight. (Psalm 5:12)

I declare the favor of God shows up every time, all the time. My life will never be the same because of the favor of God that is firmly planted in it. This is the time of God's favor in my life and I declare I receive NOTHING LESS!

Thank you, Father, for your favor of God. In Jesus' name, Amen.

Notes:

____

____

____

____

____

____

____

Finances: Wholeness and Increase

In the name of Jesus, I declare I walk boldly in my covenant rights with God. I have the peace of God; therefore, I am whole and complete in every area. I declare; peace guides me to God's favor and activates God's promise in my life. I declare; nothing is missing or broken in my life. My peace in God provides me the reassurance that I am empowered by God to succeed in everything I do.

Father, in the Name of Jesus I declare financial wholeness and increase over my finances this day, I claim the windows of heaven will pour out a financial blessing for my life that I must make room to receive (Mal. 3:10). Thank You Father, I declare my mind is alert, I hear Your voice and I will do what you call me to do to walk in Favor.

Thank You, I receive NOW, financial opportunities opening for me, my husband, and family. Father, your word says, give and it shall be given unto you, and I have (Luke 6:38).

I declare I will always operate with nothing missing and nothing lacking! Everything I may need you, Father will bring those who will have the power and authority to sow into my life. I stand in expectancy daily for the Spirit of God to speak to men and women concerning favoring to me, and in the name of Jesus those to whom the Spirit of God has designated to show me favor, they are free to obey and give to me. Jobs, Contracts, pay increase, more hours, I declare It's all mine in Jesus name!

In Jesus' Name, I declare every need is met with heaven's best. Father, you promised that You would supply all my need according to your riches in glory by Christ Jesus (Phil. 4:19). So, I thank You Father, my husband, family and I live with Gods best, and we enjoy the best in every area of my life.

Now, Satan, I bind your activity in my life and my thoughts, I loose the angels, the ministering spirits of God to minister for me and bring in the necessary finances so that I may continue to finance my household and the kingdom of God (Ps. 91:11).

I thank You Father, I have the abundance of peace, the abundance of joy, the abundance of patience, the abundance of temperance and the abundance of goodness, and an abundance of money (Gal. 5:22).

I call in great increase from the north, south, east, and west. My prosperity is a finished work in Jesus and I believe I receive it RIGHT now, In Jesus' name. Amen.

Notes:

____

____

____

____

____

____

____

Forgiveness: Making Wrong Mistakes (2)

In the name of Jesus, I declare I walk boldly in my covenant rights with God. I have the peace of God; therefore, I am whole and complete in every area. I declare; peace guides me to God's favor and activates God's promise in my life. I declare; nothing is missing or broken in my life. My peace in God provides me the reassurance that I am empowered by God to succeed in everything I do.

Father in the name of Jesus, I declare that I am supernaturally renewed from any wrong or bad decision I have made. Thank you, Lord, for showing me grace and mercy even in the midst of this current situation. Your word says that in Romans 5:20-21 that where sin and wrong doing abounds, your grace and mercy abounds much more.

I thank you Lord, for being a very present help in this time of trouble (Ps. 46:1). Thank you, Lord, for giving me your strength when I am weak. I declare now, that you have made me strong.

In my wrong, thank you father for covering me. I declare that you Lord are my sun and my shield, you bestow grace, favor, and mercy to me and my future **glorifies** you (Ps. 27:1). Thank you Lord for blotting out my transgression and placing me in a place to accept responsibility but also to have a favorable outcome.

I declare, this mistake will not take me off the path of righteousness that you have placed me on (Prov. 12:28). I will achieve my goals, I will make a mark in the lives I encounter, see great success and promotion in my life, and I will be a witness of Gods mercy, grace and favor.

Thank you, Lord, for your tender grace and mercy that is new every morning (Lam. 2:22-23).

In Jesus' name, Amen.

Notes:

Forgiveness: Past Hurts

In the name of Jesus, I declare I walk boldly in my covenant rights with God. I have the peace of God; therefore, I am whole and complete in every area. I declare; peace guides me to God's favor and activates God's promise in my life. I declare; nothing is missing or broken in my life. My peace in God provides me the reassurance that I am empowered by God to succeed in everything I do.

Father, in the Name of Jesus, I declare I make a fresh commitment to You to live in peace and harmony, not only with my husband, but also with my friends, associates, neighbors, co-workers, family, and even those who have hurt me in the past. Your word says in Matthew 6:14 that if I forgive people their trespasses, their reckless and willful sins, leaving them, letting them go and giving up resentment towards them, you Lord, will forgive me of my sins.

So, this day, I declare, I let go of all bitterness, resentment, envying, strife, hurt feelings, wrong doing towards me, and unkindness in any form. I decide this day I will not give any place to the devil by holding aught against my brother in Jesus' Name.

Thank you, Father God, for reminding me that past hurts are not a prediction of my future. My past remains in the past and will never destroy or compromise the future you have for me Father.

I declare, I forgive all those who hurt me in my past and I also receive my forgiveness from Christ. By faith, I receive it, having assurance that I am cleansed from all unrighteousness through Jesus Christ.

Thank you Lord that you are dealing with those who hurt me and you will show them your love, your mercy and loving-kindness as they seek you for guidance and forgiveness (Col. 3:12). From this moment on, I purpose to walk in love, forgiveness, and your joy. I will seek peace with all men and women on the earth.

Thank you Lord that love and your forgiving power flows liberally into the lives of everyone I know. I declare, I am filled with and abound in the fruits of righteousness which bring glory and honor unto You, Lord, in Jesus' Name (Phil. 1:11). So be it! In Jesus Name, Amen.

Notes:

Forgiveness: Self

In the name of Jesus, I declare I walk boldly in my covenant rights with God. I have the peace of God; therefore, I am whole and complete in every area. I declare; peace guides me to God's favor and activates God's promise in my life. I declare; nothing is missing or broken in my life. My peace in God provides me the reassurance that I am empowered by God to succeed in everything I do.

Father, In the name of Jesus, I declare that I will not put down, shame, or be overly disappointed in myself. For I am your handiwork, created in Christ Jesus to do good works, which you Lord prepared in advance for us to do. (Eph. 2:10) I declare I am a work in progress and where I stood a year ago, I know I am a better me today because of your word.

I declare I am useful and helpful to my family, my husband, my community, and the church body. I am tenderhearted, compassionate, understanding and forgiving of others as you commanded in your work. (Col. 3:12) This same forgiveness, love, compassion and mercy I extend to others, I will also extend to myself.

Thank you, Lord, I confession as it is written in Eph. 4:32 God has forgiven me, I will shall follow his lead and forgive myself also. Thank you, Lord, I am not hot tempered to hold myself to unrealistic expectations of perfection. However, I will strive to be who God has created me to be. Lord you said, you Create in me a pure heart and you renew a steadfast spirit within me (Ps. 51:10).

I declare I move forward today, to make a positive impact in my life, the life of my family, and in the body of Christ. I declare any ungodly spirits or actions that attempt to bring me into remembrance of my past will be declared and rendered void, In Jesus Name. For my eyes stay open and watchful that I may meditate on your promises. (Ps. 119:148)

Thank you Lord for being my example of forgiveness. I declare, I will never again punish myself but will repent from negative and bad decision which allows me to move forward in the promises of God.

Today, I forgive myself. I let the hurt, pain, frustration, anger, bad attitude, and lies about never being success go in Jesus Name. I declare I am more than a conqueror because you Lord, you love me (Rom. 8:37).

I declare, I can do all this through him who gives me strength (Phil. 4:13) And because forgiveness of self is included in "all things" I declare it is and shall be done.

Thank you, Lord, for providing me with your awesome love and grace that allows me to move forward free from the stain of my past. I receive forgiveness now, In Jesus Name Amen.

Notes:

____

____

____

____

Health and Healing

In the name of Jesus, I declare I walk boldly in my covenant rights with God. I have the peace of God; therefore, I am whole and complete in every area. I declare; peace guides me to God's favor and activates God's promise in my life. I declare; nothing is missing or broken in my life. My peace in God provides me the reassurance that I am empowered by God to succeed in everything I do.

Lord, I confess your word over my husband, my children, my family and myself this day. I know if I cry out to you, you will heal me. So, thank you for keeping me healthy and sickness far from me. (Ps. 30:2)

I declare, I shall not die but live, I shall declare the works of your hand lord and it is always good. I believe that Your Word will never return to me void, but will always accomplish what I speak it shall do (Ps. 118:17; Isa. 55:11). Therefore, I believe in the Name of Jesus that I, my husband, and my family are healthy healed, according to 1 Peter 2:24 which says Jesus himself took all our infirmities and bore our sicknesses.

Thank you, Father, for you healing word, with great boldness and confidence I say now, the authority that written Word is in my mouth, and on my lips and we are redeemed from the curse of sickness, and I refuse to tolerate its symptoms (Gal. 3:13).

Satan, I speak to you in the Name of Jesus and say that your principalities, powers, your spirits that rule this present darkness, and your spiritual wickedness are bound from operating against me, my husband, and my family in any way (Eph. 6:12).

Now, Father, as a result of my love, honor, and respect for you, I declare I will dwell in the promise of Your word that the angel of the Lord will continue to encamp themselves around me and delivers me from every evil work (Ps. 91:11). No evil shall befall me, no plague or calamity shall come near my dwelling (Ps. 91:10).

I confess the Word of God abides in me and delivers to me perfect soundness of mind and wellness in body and spirit. That Word of God is medication to my life and the law of God's Spirit operates in me (2 Tim. 1:7).

Thank you, lord, Jesus is the High Priest of my confession, and I hold fast to my confession of faith in Your Word. I stand immovable and fixed in full assurance that I, my husband, and my family have health and healing now in the Name of Jesus' Amen (1 Cor. 15:58).

Notes:

____

____

____

____

____

____

Husband: Declaration

In the name of Jesus, I declare I walk boldly in my covenant rights with God. I have the peace of God; therefore, I am whole and complete in every area. I declare; peace guides me to God's favor and activates God's promise in my life. I declare; nothing is missing or broken in my life. My peace in God provides me the reassurance that I am empowered by God to succeed in everything I do.

Father in the name of Jesus, I boldly declare I am far more precious than jewels to my husband and my value is clearly express in love to my husband (Prov. 31:10)! Thank you, Lord, the heart of my husband trusts in me confidently and relies on and believes in me completely, thank you Lord my husband has no lack of anything because I stand with him totally (Prov. 31:11).

Father, I declare that this day I will comfort, encourage, and do my husband only good as long as there is life within him. I declare will strengthen and love him fully -- spiritual, mental, and physical as long as I have breath in my body (Prov. 31:12).

I declare my husband and I taste and see that our gain from work with and for God is good (Ps. 34:8)! My husband is known as a success in everything he puts his hand to. He is strong, he is intelligent, he is capable of completing and doing everything you have called him to do. I declare everything his hands touch shall prosper (2 Cor. 9:11)! I declare the words out of his mouth will be good, will be edifying, will be fruitful, and those word will do us good all the days of our life (Eph. 4:29).

Thank you, Lord, I declare that I am secure and at peace in knowing that my family is ready for the future. I declare, when

I open my mouth ONLY skillful and Godly wisdom will come out, I declare I will use my tongue for peace, kindness and love toward my husband. He will be edified through my words, there won't be anything out of my mouth that will destroy him.

Thank you, Lord, I declare I am a peaceful wife (Eph. 4:29; Matt. 5:9)!

Thank you, Lord, my husband praises me, saying only good things towards me, thank you **F**ather God, I declare my husband who is the head over me will love me like you have called him to love me, thank you Lord, I declare we walk together in peace all the days of our lives. (1Peter 3:7; Eph. 5:31).

Thank you, Lord, for I believe I receive everything I pray and confess the word will bring it to past in Jesus' name, Amen (Mark 11:24).

Notes:

____

____

____

____

____

____

Husband: Love, Honor, Respect

In the name of Jesus, I declare I walk boldly in my covenant rights with God. I have the peace of God; therefore, I am whole and complete in every area. I declare; peace guides me to God's favor and activates God's promise in my life. I declare; nothing is missing or broken in my life. My peace in God provides me the reassurance that I am empowered by God to succeed in everything I do.

Thank you **L**ord that I operate in the spiritual gifts of love, honor, and respect toward my husband. I will always treat my husband with the fruit of your spirit (Prov. 31:11-12).

Thank you, Lord, that I am patient and kind towards my husband. I do not envy or boast. I am not proud, rude, self-seeking, or easily angered. I keep no record of wrongs in my marriage. I do not delight in evil, but rejoice ONLY in truth (1 Cor. 13:4-8).

I always protect and trust in my husband, he is the god-head of my house, and I will respect him as such. I will stay in hope and persevere because I know love and God's word never fails.

I confess, I will encourage my husband and build him up only, I will never use my words to tear him down. I will not pay back wrong for wrong, but I will always seek to be kind to him. I pray continually for him, never giving up on him, and continuously giving thanks in no matter our present circumstances (1Thes. E5:18).

My husband is a man of honor, a man after God's heart, seeks wisdom from god, wealthy in love, patience, kindness, knowledge and money (Prov. 3:13).

Thank you **L**ord for the man you have given me. Thank you that you have given me the strength to respect and reverence my husband, to notice him, regard him, prefer him, and esteem him. Thank you lord that I love and admire him (Eph. 5:33).

Therefore, I believe I receive what I pray and confess and your word will bring it to pass right now. In Jesus' name, Amen (Matt. 21:22)!

Notes:

Husband: Marriage Harmony

In the name of Jesus, I declare I walk boldly in my covenant rights with God. I have the peace of God; therefore, I am whole and complete in every area. I declare; peace guides me to God's favor and activates God's promise in my life. I declare; nothing is missing or broken in my life. My peace in God provides me the reassurance that I am empowered by God to succeed in everything I do.

Father, in the Name of Jesus, it is written in Your Word that Your love is shed abroad in our hearts by the Holy Spirit Who is given to us (Rom. 5:15). Because You are in us, we acknowledge that your love reigns supreme in my life and my marriage.

I believe that your love is displayed in full expression in my marriage, we walk together in truth, making us perfect for every good work to do Your will for our marriage. My marriage is successful and is pleasing in Your sight (Ps. 19:14).

I declare we live and conduct our marriage and ourselves honorably and becomingly before God. I declare I esteem my marriage as precious, worthy, and in great peace. We commit ourselves to live in mutual harmony and on one accord with each other- delighting in each other, being there for each other, loving on each other, and working towards peace and success with each other (Eph. 4:32).

We are of the same mind and united in spirit because you Lord (1 Cor. 2:16).

Father, we believe and say that we are gentle, compassionate, courteous, tenderhearted, and humble-minded towards each other (Eph. 4:2).

We seek peace, and it keeps our hearts in quietness and assurance. Because we follow after love and dwell in peace, our prayers are not hindered in any way, in the Name of Jesus (Rom. 12: 18).

We are heirs together of the grace of God. Our marriage grows stronger day by day in the bond of unity-- because it is founded on Your Word and rooted and grounded in Your love (Rom. 8:17).

We decree this day, we have a marriage made in heaven! It is prosperous, it is WHOLE, there is nothing missing or lacking in our marriage. We are happy, and joyful with each other. Father, we thank You for the performance of it all (2 Cor. 9:8).

We believe we receive what we have prayed and confessed in Jesus' mighty Name, Amen (Mark 11:24).

Notes:

Husband: No Weapon Formed Shall Prosper

In the name of Jesus, I declare I walk boldly in my covenant rights with God. I have the peace of God; therefore, I am whole and complete in every area. I declare; peace guides me to God's favor and activates God's promise in my life. I declare; nothing is missing or broken in my life. My peace in God provides me the reassurance that I am empowered by God to succeed in everything I do.

Father, in the Name of Jesus, I take Your Word and speak it out of my mouth and say that I have faith that I am a capable, intelligent, patient, and virtuous woman who is able to stand against the tricks of the enemy concerning my marriage (John 10:10).

No lie, trick, wrong information, unbecoming activities, will stand in my marriage. Thank you, Jesus, for giving me authority in my mouth to shut down these attacks with Your word. Your word says, GREATER is he that is in me, then he that is in the world, lord you said that you have given us all wisdom and understanding, how to handle every situation in our lives (1 John 4;4). Thank you lord that you said YOU hold success in store for the upright and YOU are the shield to those who walk blameless in you… Thank you Lord that is ME, that is my husband and that is my family!

Satan in the Name of Jesus, I rebuke YOU, your tricks, and your lies that you tell me or my husband about our relationship. Satan, you are defeated TODAY, RIGTH NOW in EVERYTHING you do, and I put you where you belong UNDER our feet (Rom. 16:20)! Thank you lord that I can put a DEMAND on the Word of God RIGHT now, and your word says ANYTHING I pray and confess, if I believe I receive it I will have, YES, it's MINE (Mark 11:24)!

So, I have peace in my home, I have joy in my marriage, I have YEARS of lasting LOVE with my husband, I have understanding and forgiveness in my marriage. We are BLESSED going in and going out (Deut. 28:1-68)! My husband and I are victorious in everything we put our hands to. Satan, I serve you Notice, you cannot and will not have my marriage, my husband, my family or me, and you are a defeated foe (Rev. 12:11).

In the name of Jesus, I know I receive what I have confessed in Jesus' name, Amen!

Notes:

____

____

____

____

____

____

____

Husband: Thankfulness

In the name of Jesus, I declare I walk boldly in my covenant rights with God. I have the peace of God; therefore, I am whole and complete in every area. I declare; peace guides me to God's favor and activates God's promise in my life. I declare; nothing is missing or broken in my life. My peace in God provides me the reassurance that I am empowered by God to succeed in everything I do.

In the name of Jesus, I declare, I am a virtuous woman of GOD and the PERFECT WIFE for my husband. I am the CROWN he cherishes and a GIFT to his life (Prov. 31-10-12). Thank you, Lord, for my LIFE and for my husband. Thanks **F**ather my husband loves me unconditionally, thank you **L**ord he honors and respects me daily. Thank you Lord that we stay committed to each other and our relationship in good times and bad; he desires ONLY me all the days of his life (Prov. 31:10-31; 1 Peter 3:7)).

I declare my husband is humble and upright in all his daily interactions. Thank you Lord He operates in INTEGRITY, he is a man of WISDOM, His word is impeccable, thank you **L**ord he is respected among his peers to speak wisdom and sound reason into their lives (Prov. 31:23).

Thank you, Lord, our marriage is missing nothing, is in need of nothing, and is in lack of nothing no matter what it looks like. Thank you, thank you, thank you Lord for Your word, thank you Lord that it brings us TRUTH, and OUR final authority (Heb. 12:2).

Thank you Lord for supplying ALL our needs according to YOUR riches in glory, thanks for witty inventions and super-natural insight you placed in my husband heart. I declare that my husband is successful in EVERYTHING he seeks to do;

his business, on his job, or in any future ventures he encounters, HE WINS, which means WE WIN (Phil. 4:19).

Thank you, Father, that he is bless in season and out, going and coming. He shall have success all the days of his life. Father God, I stand this morning, in LOVE, knowing that your word NEVER FAILS (2 Cor. 9:8; Josh. 21:45)!

Thank you, Father, that your word shall never depart from my husband's mouth, his confessions and his declarations shall produce good and NEVER evil. Because my husband mediates on the word of God day and night, and he is led by Your spirit and your spirit alone, good shall follow him all the days of his life (Josh. 1:8). Thank you, Jesus!

Lord, I rebuke Satan right now in the name of Jesus. No hurt, un-forgiveness, anxiety, depression, fear, strife or sadness of any kind will touch his life. Our marriage will operate in Peace, Joy, Hope, Forgiveness, Unconditional love, and prosperity (Gal. 5:22)

Thank you, Father, that I never dishonor my husband or my marriage and he will never dishonor me, I will ONLY SPEAK LIFE INTO HIM, BLESS HIM, PRAISE HIM, and DO HIM GOOD all the days of his life (Eph. 4:29). Thank you Lord for giving me the STRENGHT and desire to LOVE LIKE YOU, to server like YOU, to forgive like You (Col. 3:13).

Thank you Lord that even in the mist of trails, I call us BLESSED, HIGHLY FAVORED and ANNOINTED BY YOU (1 John 2:20). I declare I will never cave in, quiet, or GIVE UP on your word, my marriage, my husband, or my family.

In Jesus' Name, I believe I received everything I have confessed, Amen (Mark 11:2).

Notes:

Notes:

I Believe Only

In the name of Jesus, I declare I walk boldly in my covenant rights with God. I have the peace of God; therefore, I am whole and complete in every area. I declare; peace guides me to God's favor and activates God's promise in my life. I declare; nothing is missing or broken in my life. My peace in God provides me the reassurance that I am empowered by God to succeed in everything I do.

In the name of Jesus, I declare you Lord God are my strength, refuge, and my shelter from any and all of life's storms (Jer. 16-19). Thank you, Father, for the rest I find in you, knowing that the good work that you have started in me will be finish (Phil. 1:6).

This day, I declare my life will continually be a life of belief. I believe the word of God ONLY, and I declare I will not trust in what I see, feel, or hear. I trust Gods word as my final authority (Ps. 31:14-15).

In the name of Jesus, I declare, I have authority over my thought life daily. Although, I live in the flesh, I declare I will not war against things that are trying me according to the flesh. I will war in the spirit for I know my spiritual warfare is mighty and God will stand with me to overthrow and destroy any evil forces that is attempting to bring destructive strongholds into my life (Eph. 6:10-20).

I declare that my belief in God's word has afforded me a life of PEACE, JOY, FORGIVENESS, RESTORATION, and PROSPEITY (James 2:19)!

I declare I am an overcomer. I overcome the devil in every confrontation or trick he tries to throw at me, he never overcomes me. I overcome him by the blood of the lamb, and the word of my testimony (1John 5:4-5).

I declare I believe GOD ONLY, and his words are my assurance, my peace, my joy, my wisdom and my guidance. I declare, a voice of another I will never follow (John 10:27).

I believe, God is for me so WHO can be against me (Rom. 8:31)? I am one with my Father! He stands ready to show up on my behalf. He supplies my all my needs because He is for me (Phil. 4:19)!

I declare all my sufficiency is in God. All authority in heaven and on earth resides in the name of Jesus and I have been given authority to use it (John 14:12).

I declare and I believe God's word ONLY. I am a believer, I only BELIEVE, no longer doubt (James 1:16). In Jesus' name, Amen.

Notes:

____

____

____

____

____

Joy

In the name of Jesus, I declare I walk boldly in my covenant rights with God. I have the peace of God; therefore, I am whole and complete in every area. I declare; peace guides me to God's favor and activates God's promise in my life. I declare; nothing is missing or broken in my life. My peace in God provides me the reassurance that I am empowered by God to succeed in everything I do.

In the name of Jesus, I declare I have joy. The joy of the Lord is my strength and it receive God's Joy in my heart right now (Neh. 8:10). Thank you Lord for every spirit of depression, anxiety, fear, frustration is broken over my life. Those spirits have no right or authority in me or around me because I am the Child of the Most High God (1 Cor. 15:28; Eph. 4:6).

I declare that weeping may endure for the night but joy always cometh in the morning (Ps. 30:5). I declare right now I live in joy. The more Word I meditate on and consume, the more joy I have. I declare, the joy of the Lord is my strength!

In the name of Jesus, I thank you for giving me a garment of praise for the spirit of heaviness

(Isa. 61:3). You said I can cast my cares upon you because you care for me so today, right now, I caste, the heaviness of fear, torment, pain, lost, not being enough, selfishness, loneliness, stress, anxiety, and worry on you because I know I was not created to carry them (1Peter 5:7). I declare, I have the joy of the Lord and a joyful spirit. The Joy that I have is unspeakable.

Thank you Lord the weight and heaviness of bondage and cares of this world have been lifted from me, in Jesus name. I declare I have Gods Joy and a lightness about me (Ex. 20:2; Rom. 12:12).

Today, I eat at the table that has been prepared for me in the presence of my enemies and I am in Joy and Peace (Ps. 23:5). I declare, what has been stolen shall be returned, in Jesus name. What the devil thought he would use to destroy me, shall NOW be given back to me sevenfold (Prov. 6:31)

Now in the name of Jesus let the return begin. My Joy, Peace, Confidence, trust, and prosperity; I call it here NOW! From this point on I trouble my trouble with joy (Phil. 4:4).

In Jesus' name, Amen.

Notes:

____

____

____

____

____

____

____

____

Peace

In the name of Jesus, I declare I walk boldly in my covenant rights with God. I have the peace of God; therefore, I am whole and complete in every area. I declare; peace guides me to God's favor and activates God's promise in my life. I declare; nothing is missing or broken in my life. My peace in God provides me the reassurance that I am empowered by God to succeed in everything I do.

Thank You Lord, for Your peace that passes all understanding (Phil. 4:7). I declare no matter what I may be facing, I don't have to fear, because You are always with me (Josh. 1:9).

I declare, I will not fret or have anxiety about anything, but in every circumstance and situation, by prayer and petition, with thanksgiving, I continue to make my requests known to God and he will answer, because He loves me (Matt 6:25-34).

I declare I make a decision now to use God's promise of peace to set my thoughts and atmosphere. My heart will not be troubled. I hold on to my peace in God. I guard my mind and my heart with the peace of God. I declare now that I will no longer ignore my internal system of peace. Peace is and will continue to be my umpire. Peace is my friend and peace will direct me into the place of calm with God (1 John 14:27).

Satan, I rebuke your attempts to interrupt, disturb, or challenge my peace. You have not authority or Place in my life, mind, body, or thoughts. Anxiety, Fear, torment, confusion, and dread you MUST GO NOW! I declare, you are defeated, and YOU lose because I WIN in Christ every day, every min, every hour. Christ is in me, the Hope of Glory (Jude 1:9; James 4:7).

I declare, I'm not moved by what I see, feel, or hear. I only let the peace of God rule in my heart and thankfulness will stay on my lips (Phil. 4:6).

I declare right now, in the midst of trouble, heartache, frustration, confusion, I will say: "Peace, be still." In my finances "Peace be still." In my marriage "Peace be still." In every area of my life "Peace be still." I declare a great calm over my life (Mark 4:39).

Thank you Lord for keeping me in perfect peace, because my mind is fixed on you (Isa. 26:3)! Thank you Lord for your peace which transcends all understanding (Phil. 4:7).

In Jesus' name. Amen.

Notes:

____

____

____

____

____

____

Redeemed from Lack

In the name of Jesus, I declare I walk boldly in my covenant rights with God. I have the peace of God; therefore, I am whole and complete in every area. I declare; peace guides me to God's favor and activates God's promise in my life. I declare; nothing is missing or broken in my life. My peace in God provides me the reassurance that I am empowered by God to succeed in everything I do.

In the name of Jesus, I declare Christ has redeemed me from the curse of the law. Thank you Lord for redeeming me from poverty, lack, sickness, spiritual death, and destruction. Thank you Lord that I am the apple of your eye and you make sure I lack nothing (Gal. 3:13).

Thank you, Lord, for your word which gives me beauty for Ashes. For poverty, Lord you have given me wealth, for sickness you have given me health, for death you have given me eternal life and I shall lack no good thing (Isa. 61:1-3).

I declare, I my delight is in you Lord and you will give me the desires of my heart (Ps. 37:4). I declare, I lack no good thing, for God will not withhold good from his children, and I am a child of God (Ps. 34:10).

I boldly confess, I have given and it is given back to me good measure, pressed down, shaken together, running over shall man give unto my bosom. For with what measure I mete it is measured unto me (Luke 6:38).

I declare, I sow continuously into the ministry of God bountifully. Therefore, I shall reap bountifully. I declare, I am a cheerfully giver and my God has made all grace abound towards me and having all things do abound to all good works (2 Cor. 9:7).

I declare, there is no lack in the life of my husband, children, or family for my God has supplied all my needs according to His riches in glory. Lord you are my Shepherd and I do not want for anything (Phil. 4:19).

Thank you, Lord, Jesus was made poor that I, through His poverty might have abundance. For He came that I might have life and have it more abundantly (John 10:10). I have received abundance of grace and the gift of righteousness do reign as king in life by Christ Jesus.

Thank you Lord for taking pleasure in my prosperity. Thank you, lord, Abraham's blessings are mine (Gen. 12:1-3)! IN JESUS' NAME AMEN!

Notes:

____

____

____

____

____

____

____

Releasing Selfishness

In the name of Jesus, I declare I walk boldly in my covenant rights with God. I have the peace of God; therefore, I am whole and complete in every area. I declare; peace guides me to God's favor and activates God's promise in my life. I declare; nothing is missing or broken in my life. My peace in God provides me the reassurance that I am empowered by God to succeed in everything I do.

I declare **F**ather that your goodness and your mercy follows me, all the days of my life and I have the ability to be selfless in my marriage and in my life (Ps. 23:6).

Thank you Lord for transforming my character to be more like you! Thank you Lord for revealing the selfish areas in my life in order to shine your light of healing on those areas and You will assist me in developing a RIGHT spirit within me (2 Tim. 3:16).

I declare, the fruit of selfishness CAN NOT remain in me. I rebuke it now: I am NOT a lover of only myself, I am not covetous, a boaster, proud, disobedient, unthankful, unholy, or self-seeking. I rebuke them all in Jesus name (2 Tim. 3:1-5).

I rebuke moodiness and complaining, Laziness and irresponsibility, I rebuke being EASILY angered and Never listening, I rebuke being manipulative and controlling. I rebuke every fruit of selfishness. It is not welcome in me or in my house.

Thank you **L**ord I declare, I will not seek my own will for selfish gain, but will seek the will of God for my husband and my family. I give preference to them in honor and in Godly Love.

I declare, I commit this day, I will not focus on myself at the expense of others, I will not be demanding of my needs and wants without considering the needs of the whole first. I will not judge other or my husband harshly. My feelings are NOT 1st priority, the WORD OF GOD is my Priority.

Thank you Lord that you are helping me to serve my husband in a loving way, in a selfless way, in a way that is more like you! Thank you for changing and transforming my character to be more like you and LESS like the World.

In the name of Jesus, I believe I receive everything I have prayed and confessed and I know lord you will bring it pass, In Jesus' Name, Amen (Mark 11:24).

Notes:

____

____

____

____

____

____

____

Victorious Wife

In the name of Jesus, I declare I walk boldly in my covenant rights with God. I have the peace of God; therefore, I am whole and complete in every area. I declare; peace guides me to God's favor and activates God's promise in my life. I declare; nothing is missing or broken in my life. My peace in God provides me the reassurance that I am empowered by God to succeed in everything I do.

Father, I thank You my mind and my spirit is renewed by your word daily (Ps. 51:20). My hope and expectations are from You are firmly planted in you.

I declare I daily receive the manifestation of Your Word in my life and I thank You for beginning a good work in me (Phil.1:6). I stand firm knowing I am a capable, intelligent, virtuous woman, and I win in every situation I face. I live the overcomer's life (1 John 4:4-5). I live in daily expectation of abundance for my life. I am a victorious woman of God.

I declare, every need in my life is met with Gods best! I have a sound mind, I am healthy and fit, and I live a long life because I am redeemed from destruction and the curse of the law

(Gal. 3:13). I declare I walk in divine health and healing. It is my covenant right as a believer. I dwell in the secret place of the Most High and no plague shall come near my husband, children, family, or dwelling (Ps. 91:1-16).

The devil is rebuked concerning every part of my life and all that concerns me; he shall not destroy my relationships, marriage, and job. Neither shall he come near the favor of God on my life (James 4:7). The Lord redeems my life from destruction; I overcome every obstacle with my faith.

I declare my mind is alert; my body is full of strength all the days of my life (Ps. 103:4).

I declare, I live a life of purpose with fulfillment and in victory; I am a blessing to my husband, my family, my friends, and to the kingdom of God (1 Cor. 15-57). Thank you, Lord, I will stay FAITHFUL to your word, I will not, stop, cave in, or quit in the mist of the process - NO MATTER what it looks like or EVEN when FEAR shows its face (2 Tim. 1:7). I will stand steadfast, unmovable, trusting and knowing you are my ROCK and my salvation (Ps. 62:1-12); your word I will confess daily, because I know anything I pray in your word, if I believe that I RECEIVE IT and I shall have it (Mark 11:24)!

Thank you, Father, ~ The blessings of Abraham are MINE! Thank you, Lord, (Gen. 12:1-20):

Your will Lead me into a blessed and prosperous land

You will make me a GREAT nation

You will bless me and my children

You will make my name great

And, I will be a blessing to other. It is MY inheritance as a CHILD OF GOD, to be successful, prosperous, and full of wisdom and knowledge on how to see the manifestation in my life. And, I believe I receive everything I have prayed and confessed, and I am confident that the lord's word will bring it all to pass in Jesus' name, Amen (John 14:13).

Notes:

Notes:

Walk by Faith, Not by Sight

In the name of Jesus, I declare I walk boldly in my covenant rights with God. I have the peace of God; therefore, I am whole and complete in every area. I declare; peace guides me to God's favor and activates God's promise in my life. I declare; nothing is missing or broken in my life. My peace in God provides me the reassurance that I am empowered by God to succeed in everything I do.

Father, In the name of Jesus, I declare today, I will walk by faith and not by sight or in fear (2 Cor. 5:7). Today I choose life and your life father that is full of joy, peace, and abundance (Rom. 15-13).

Thank you, Father, for always being with me and never leaving my side. I declare my eyes are open to see your directions and path, and to recognize the trick of the enemy (Ps. 119-105). Thank you, Lord, my ears are tuned to your voice and a voice of another I will never follow (John 10:27).

Thank you, Lord, I declare this day my faith is strong, bold, and relentlessly great. I stand in faith from this day moving forward, NEVER getting weary or quitting on the promises of God (Gal. 6:9).

I declare I will Never again, base my decision on my thoughts, my circumstances, my own logic and understanding, or what I see. No, from this day forward, I stand in my God Faith. Faith in the word of God, the that faith that moves mountains and changes lives, the faith that raises people from the dead, that heals the sick and depress, that faith that commands greatness in the lives of those I love and it manifest. Yes, today, I stand in Faith that parts the sea and causes debts to be cancelled, and financial increase to show up. My faith is real, my faith is active, and my faith is working for me and in me (Rom 1:17).

Never again will I walk out my day, without standing firmly planted in my God kind of Faith (Ps. 1:3).

Thank you, Lord, I know faith comes by hearing and hearing the word of God, and I will continue to build my faith standing on a solid foundation (Rom. 10:17).

I declare, I am surrounded by protective angels that are encamped all around me (Ps. 34:7). Thank you, Father, for the hedge of protection that You bring in response to my faith (Job 1:10). I declare, I have a strong unbreakable faith! I shall see the manifestation of every promise made in your Word Lord. I declare every promise will shall come to pass. I declare and decree I will stand firm in my faith, not wavering at the promises of God because what is before me. In Jesus Name, Amen.

Notes:

____

____

____

____

____

____

Wife: Blessed to be ME (Self-Esteem)

In the name of Jesus, I declare I walk boldly in my covenant rights with God. I have the peace of God; therefore, I am whole and complete in every area. I declare; peace guides me to God's favor and activates God's promise in my life. I declare; nothing is missing or broken in my life. My peace in God provides me the reassurance that I am empowered by God to succeed in everything I do.

I declare, my life has purpose, meaning, and is bigger than what I see. Thank you Lord for making me unique and special just for your use. I am happy and full of joy because you loved me and there is nobody on earth exactly like me or capable of being the women, wife, sister, and friend you created me to be (Deut. 7:6)

I declare I am strong, wise, confident, bold, and fearless in you Father. Nothing and No one will steal my light of Greatness. Thank You that I have been chosen by you for a great purpose and call and I walk in it fully this day. In you father, you have made me confident (Eph. 1:4).

Thank you, Lord, I declare, I am created in Your image and your likeness. I am happy with who you made me to be. Every unique style, word choice, and inner difference, I accept and love. I appreciate me and I am enough (Gen. 1:27).

Thank You **F**ather for seeing the good in me, the help I can be to others and the answer my life will be to those I encounter. Thank you lord for helping me to grow into the greatest women I can be, destined to win and to never lose, designed to see and be great for your kingdom because I am your workmanship (Gen. 1:31; Eph. 2:10).

Thank you, Lord, I am fearfully and wonderfully made by you and I know all your works are marvelous. Thank you, Father, for calling me your treasure – for placing value in me. I am very valuable to you, the kingdom of God, and to my family (Ps. 139:14; Exod. 19:5).

Thank You Lord for reminding me that I am blessed, favored, and called a marvelous treasure in your sight Thank you for loving me with everlasting love. Because of You – my life is filled with favor, joy, love, and your many blessings (Jer. 31:3).

Today, I declare, I am blessed, blessed to be me uniquely authentically me! In Jesus Name, Amen.

Notes:

____

____

____

____

____

____

____

Wife: Courage and Confidence

In the name of Jesus, I declare I walk boldly in my covenant rights with God. I have the peace of God; therefore, I am whole and complete in every area. I declare; peace guides me to God's favor and activates God's promise in my life. I declare; nothing is missing or broken in my life. My peace in God provides me the reassurance that I am empowered by God to succeed in everything I do.

Thank you, Lord, I am full of courage and confidence that comes from you. This boundless confidence and trust had grown out of your word that says greater is he that is in me than he that is in the world (1 John 4:4). I am fully persuaded of your love Father, for me and I can stand firm, planted, and unmovable on your word daily.

I declare, I can do all things through Him who strengthens me. (Phil. 4:13) I am strong and courageous no matter the situation or circumstance. I will not fear nor tremble or be dismayed at circumstances or situations, for the Lord my God is with me everywhere I go (Josh. 1:9).

Satan, I rebuke your attempts to take away my courage confident in God and Myself. I put no confidence in the flesh or on outward privileges and physical advantages and external appearances, I ONLY put my confidence in Jesus Christ and his Word, therefore, I win every time.

I declare, that all things work for my good because I love God and I am called according to His purpose. I Trust in the LORD with all your heart and do not lean on your own understanding. In all your ways acknowledge Him, and I know you will make your paths straight (Rom. 8:28; Prov. 3:5-6).

I declare, I will not be afraid of ten thousands of people who may set themselves against me nor round about me because you Father God, you are my defense my shield, fortress, and you will never leave me nor forsake me (Ps. 3:6).

Thank you, Lord, I am Strong, courageous, and confident in you (Deut. 31:6). In Jesus Name, Amen.

Notes:

____

____

____

____

____

____

____

____

____

____

Wife: I am Transformed into God's Image

In the name of Jesus, I declare I walk boldly in my covenant rights with God. I have the peace of God; therefore, I am whole and complete in every area. I declare; peace guides me to God's favor and activates God's promise in my life. I declare; nothing is missing or broken in my life. My peace in God provides me the reassurance that I am empowered by God to succeed in everything I do.

Father in the name of Jesus, I am who you called me to be and I renew my mind daily in your word (Rom. 12:2). Thank you father for your promised that I am my husband good thing and a gift to his life (Prov. 18:22).

I declare, I am an excellent wife to him and he and my children call me blessed. Thank you father my husband sees my presence in his life as an honor and a blessing from you. No good thing has been withheld from him because I honor him and God in prayer daily (Col. 3:18).

I declare, every one of my weaknesses, areas of stress, or even things I don't know, will never stop our family from reaching Gods destination for our lives! Thank you lord for shinning your light on the areas that must be restored and these areas will never impact the role, director, or financial projection for our lives (Joel 2:25-26).

Thank you Lord for guiding and directing me daily to see the ungodliness that maybe shielded with emotions but are coming from my inner desires or my expectations. Thank you Lord that Your word will teach me how to surrender those issues to You for healing, correction, and guidance (Heb. 12:11).

Thank you, Father, for showing me where I am investing my attention in things that will deteriorate my relationship with my husband, children, family, and ministry.

I declare the power of Your Word will transform my motives, heart, emotions, and will so that I am the loving, understanding, forgiving, and caring wife you have called me to be

(1Cor. 13:4-8; Eph. 4:2)! Thank you Lord for coaching and guiding me relentlessly to be a wife who respects her husband in word and in deed.

Thank you, Father, for showering your tenderness, gentleness, kindness, and humility to on me and allowing me to become more like you (Gen. 1:27).

I declare, I will to be a content wife a godly wife, a wife after Gods heart who does not harass, nag, and push my husband with quarrels and fretfulness. Thank you Lord for using me to cultivate a peaceful, stress free, and caring home environment for my husband. Thank you for using me to encourage him, pray for him, love on him, bear his burdens, and reflect Your extravagant love toward him (Isa. 26:3).

Thank you Lord for giving me the complete confidence in you and Your Holy Spirit which is always at work in our marriage. In Jesus name, Amen.

Notes:

Notes:

Wife: Self Control

In the name of Jesus, I declare I walk boldly in my covenant rights with God. I have the peace of God; therefore, I am whole and complete in every area. I declare; peace guides me to God's favor and activates God's promise in my life. I declare; nothing is missing or broken in my life. My peace in God provides me the reassurance that I am empowered by God to succeed in everything I do.

Thank you Lord I am controlled not by my will or emotions but by the Holy Spirit. Thank you, Father, for your guidance and support to be more self-controlled.

I declare, I will not be hot-tempted, stirring up dissension, but I will be patient, calming all quarrels (Prov. 15:18) I declare I operate in self-control and don't allow my spirit to be unruly. I refuse to be like a city that is broken down, destroyed, and without walls. Self-control and discipline add protection to my life. (Prov. 25:28)

Thank you, Lord, I confess I seriously consider what I am doing before I do it. I will count the cost and consider the requirements. I declare I will expand prudently and I will not neglect the present duties by assuming too many new ones to my list of assignments. (Prov. 31:16)

I declare I am in control with the full guidance of the Holy Spirit to make right choices and decisions. When I commit to accomplish a task and I will keep my promise. (Eccl. 5:4) Thank you Lord I am not rash with my mouth, and my heart is not hasty to utter wrong or unacceptable word before god or to my family. (Eccl. 5:2) I will control my actions, my mood, and my thoughts with your words.

Thank you **L**ord for assisting me in not being quick in spirit to be angry or vexed. For anger and vexation develops and bosom into consequences I would rather not see in my life (Prov. 14:29). Thank you, Lord, for my confidence in you. I confess without you I can do no good thing. Thank you father that self-control is growing in me daily.

In Jesus' Name, Amen.

Notes:

Wife: Staying in Perfect Joy

In the name of Jesus, I declare I walk boldly in my covenant rights with God. I have the peace of God; therefore, I am whole and complete in every area. I declare; peace guides me to God's favor and activates God's promise in my life. I declare; nothing is missing or broken in my life. My peace in God provides me the reassurance that I am empowered by God to succeed in everything I do.

In the Name of Jesus, I declare that I have perfect Joy in my heart right now. Thank you, Father, for giving me the authority to use my mouth to confess what I desire to see in my life, heart, and home. I declare, that no matter what is going on around me or even in this world, Joy will continuously reside in my heart and the fruit of joy will be seen in my actions (Gal. 5:22).

I declare that even when difficult situations, troubled times and hurting hearts are before me, I will rise up and say, "The joy of the Lord is my strength" and joy and peace will cover me (Neh. 8:10).

I boldly confess this day that Thank You that the joy of the Lord is my strength and that You have promised that Your grace is sufficient for all eventualities. Keep us all with our hearts fixed on You and instill in our hearts joyful disposition so that we may bring comfort and cheer to those around us and be salt and light to those that are facing troubles or difficulties – this I ask in Jesus' Name, Amen. (Matt. 5:13-14).

Notes:

Wife: Staying in Perfect Joy

In the name of Jesus, I declare I walk boldly in my covenant rights with God. I have the peace of God; therefore, I am whole and complete in every area. I declare; peace guides me to God's favor and activates God's promise in my life. I declare; nothing is missing or broken in my life. My peace in God provides me the reassurance that I am empowered by God to succeed in everything I do.

In the Name of Jesus, I declare that I have perfect Joy in my heart right now. Thank you, Father, for giving me the authority to use my mouth to confess what I desire to see in my life, heart, and home. I declare, that no matter what is going on around me or even in this world, Joy will continuously reside in my heart and the fruit of joy will be seen in my actions (Gal. 5:22).

I declare that even when difficult situations, troubled times and hurting hearts are before me, I will rise up and say, "The joy of the Lord is my strength" and joy and peace will cover me (Neh. 8:10).

I boldly confess this day that Thank You that the joy of the Lord is my strength and that You have promised that Your grace is sufficient for all eventualities. Keep us all with our hearts fixed on You and instill in our hearts joyful disposition so that we may bring comfort and cheer to those around us and be salt and light to those that are facing troubles or difficulties – this I ask in Jesus Name, Amen (Matt. 5:13-14).

Notes:

Work and Job Change

In the name of Jesus, I declare I walk boldly in my covenant rights with God. I have the peace of God; therefore, I am whole and complete in every area. I declare; peace guides me to God's favor and activates God's promise in my life. I declare; nothing is missing or broken in my life. My peace in God provides me the reassurance that I am empowered by God to succeed in everything I do.

Thank you, Lord, for having good things in store for those who love you. For those who have been called according to your purpose. (Deut. 7:9)

Thank you for the gifts and talents that you have given me (1Peter 4:10). Even before I was born your hand was at work in the very fabric of my being and through my adult years you have stood by me and provided for me in good times and in times of need and crisis (Jer. 1:4-5).

I thank you now that you will lead and guide me to the right pace of employment. My heart is open father to see what you see and to hear what you hear. My spirit will lead me to the right job, making more than enough for my family. Thank you, Lord, that you are protecting my mind and my reasoning abilities. Thank you, Lord, for keeping me fully alert to your leading. My spirit is sensitive to your promptings.

Thank you Lord that you will open a door to a job which brings fulfillment and happiness in every area of my life. Thank you now that this job will not only provides for my needs but enables me to give freely to the needs of others (Phil. 4:19).

Thank you Lord that the job that is right for me, is for me and will assist me in help to build the kingdom of God.

You are the author of my life. Thank you for all you have given me, taught me, and shaped in me so far. I give you this next chapter and ask you would lead me through it (Ps. 20:4).

Lord, thanks for opening new opportunities, stretch my mind, enlarge my heart and my terrority. I give myself into your capable hands and trust that as I walk in the grace you have provided, you will open the right doors for me. Fill me with hope, faith, assurance, and confidence that as I go into every job interviews, I will walk out confident that I will be selected and I will walk into new opportunities of greatness. Thank you that I always carry within me your life, your truth, your hope and your love (Eph. 5:20). May those around me encounter something of you in all I do. In Jesus Name, Amen.

Notes:

____

____

____

____

____

____

____

Worry and Fear

In the name of Jesus, I declare I walk boldly in my covenant rights with God. I have the peace of God; therefore, I am whole and complete in every area. I declare; peace guides me to God's favor and activates God's promise in my life. I declare; nothing is missing or broken in my life. My peace in God provides me the reassurance that I am empowered by God to succeed in everything I do.

In the name of Jesus, I declare, I have a blood bought right to cast down all spiritual attacks against the promises of God. I declare, Satan has no power over me, my husband, or my family. I overcome Satan's evil trick and assignment with the word of God. Fear and worry has no authority in me, and command it to go now (Eph. 6:12).

In the name of Jesus, I declare, greater is He that is in me than he that is in the world (1John 4:4). I will not worry or fear any evil work because God is with me, his rod and staff comforts me (Ps. 23:4). I will mediate on the word of God and bring life to remove dark places in me.

I declare, my heart, thoughts, and body are far from depression and oppression. Satan's tools of fear and worry does not reside in me. Thank you, Lord, for my authority to confess the word, and say no weapon formed against me shall prosper, because, Lord, you will silence every voice that raised up against me and tries to overtake me (Isa. 54:17).

I declare, I replace fear with faith, and worry with mediation of the word. This affords me the covenant right to have everything I put my hands to, will prosper. For I am like a tree planted by the rivers of living water and I shall produce great fruit (Ps. 1:3).

Today, I boldly confess, I am delivered from fear, worry, anxiety, and every evil of this present world. It is the will of God concerning me. No evil will befall me neither shall any plague come nigh my dwelling for the Lord has given His angels charge over me and they keep me in all my ways (Ps. 91:10; Heb. 1:14).

I declare, in my pathway is life, abundance, peace, joy, favor, goodness, and prosperity. There is no death, worry, or fear in or near me (2 Tim. 1:7).

I declare, I am a doer of the Word of God and am blessed all the days of my life (James 1:22). I am an over-comer. I overcome by the blood of the lamb and the word of my testimony (Rev. 12:11).

I am submitted to God and the devil flees from me because I resist him in the name of Jesus

(James 4:7). The Word of God is forever settled in heaven. Therefore, I establish His Word upon this earth. Great is the peace of my children for they are taught by God (2Tim. 3:16-17). In Jesus Name, Amen.

Notes:

____

____

____

____

Website: www.wifetalkinc.com
Facebook: Wife Talk Inc
Twitter: WifeTalk07
Periscope: WifeTalk07

Made in the USA
Columbia, SC
27 August 2017